Extremists, Radicals & Non-Conformists...
Please Be One!

by

Roberts Liardon

2nd Printing

Extremists, Radicals &
Non-Conformists...
Please Be One!
ISBN 1-890900-08-7

Published by Embassy Publishing Co.
P.O. Box 3500
Laguna Hills, CA 92654

Contents

1

Three Titles Every Christian Should Want

But the Jews who were not persuaded, becoming envious, took some of the evil men from the marketplace, and gathering a mob, set all the city in an uproar and attacked the house of Jason, and sought to bring them out to the people. But when they did not find them, they dragged Jason and some brethren to the rulers of the city, crying out, "These who have turned the world upside down have come here too."

Acts 17:5-6 (NKJ)

Everywhere the Apostles preached in the book of Acts, there was a riot. They had developed a reputation — they were known as the ones who turned the world upside down. This should be your testimony too.

"Well, I don't want to stir up controversy."

Then you'll never be a world-shaker.

This is the problem with a lot of the Christians in the world today. They will compromise their beliefs for a piece of apple pie. Some Christians want everyone to say, "Oh, we like you, you're so wonderful."

The Apostles weren't afraid of being branded with negative titles. They knew how to handle resistance, opposition and hardship. When they preached, they hit the evil powers of the air and bucked the religious traditions of their day. They turned the world upside-down! What have you turned upside-down lately? Your Sunday afternoon roast, probably.

Three Titles Every Christian Should Want

There are three words which have been coming up in my spirit over the last few months. One is the word "extremist," the other is "radical," and the third is "non-conformist."

People don't usually like being labeled with these words, but I want to be called all three. I'll wear them as medals because these are the kinds of individuals that change history and fulfill divine destiny.

When you step out of the realm of average Christianity into the fullness of your call, people will say all kinds of things about you. You must develop an immunity to being labeled or you will shrink back from your divinely appointed position.

If you're scared of being labeled an extremist, radical, or non-conformist, this book is for you.

2

What Is An Extremist?

An extremist is someone who goes to the farthest degree — someone who is the most violent or aggressive. In the realm of Christianity, an extremist is one who exhibits the highest degree of faith and explores the greatest depths of prayer. It is the one who is the most violent or aggressive about getting people saved and healed.

An extremist is always one step away from a glorious victory or a devastating defeat — he or she lives on the "cutting-edge" of the move of God.

Disease Called Average

American Christianity is plagued with a disease called average. Christians who are infected with this disease will pressure you and try to make you feel "weird" for casting out devils, operating in the gifts of the Spirit and believing that Jesus heals today. But really, *they* are the ones who are "weird."

When I first started preaching as a teenager, my friends would say, "Well, you know, Roberts, you're a little bit strange." And I would respond, "I know I'm strange, but I'm not going to change." (At least I had that much grit.) Then, one day God rebuked me.

"Quit agreeing with a lie!" He said. "Anybody that obeys Me and My Word is normal! Those who don't — *they're* the weird ones!"

Don't Fit In, Stand Out!

Many churches are scared of leaving the common ground of average Christianity. They are embracing the spirit of the world and attempting to "fit-in" because they're scared of being labeled and rejected by society.

If you fit in, you're already out of the will of God! Jesus didn't fit into the system. Paul didn't fit into the system, Peter didn't fit into the system. If you obey the Holy Spirit and the Bible, you won't fit into the system either!

"Is the Lord against the system?"

He's against any system that violates His will and purposes. If the system promotes and advances the will of God, He'll bless it. But if the system opposes His will, or has a wrong type of control in it, He will call those who are listening to His Spirit out from among it.

Backslidden Christians

If all your Christianity is displayed behind the four walls of your church, then you're not an extremist, you're a backslider. You can backslide while you're singing Amazing Grace and praying in tongues, my friend.

Charles Finney, a revivalist who lived in the mid 1800s, said, "Some people like to live close to the sound of chapel bells, but I would rather build a mission one yard from the gate of hell."

Now that's called extreme.

The Negative & Positive Side Of "Extreme"

Another definition of extreme is: *the worst or the best that can exist.* David Koresh and Jim Jones lived on the negative side of the word extreme. They were extreme in the wrong direction and the devil accommodated their error.

If I'm going to be called an extremist, I want it to be because I'm extreme in the right direction. Nowadays, if you believe that the Lord wants to heal everybody, you're considered an extremist. If you believe that God wants to prosper you and give you an abundant life, then you've really gone too far. It's getting to the place in America where you're considered an extremist for simply believing and obeying the Bible. If you're going to call me an extremist for believing these things, then I'll proudly wear the label.

Jesus Went A Little Farther

In Matthew chapter 26, we find a scriptural definition of the word "extreme." Verse 36 says:

Then Jesus came with them to a place called Gethsemane, and said to the disciples, "Sit here while I go and pray over there." And He took with Him Peter and the two sons of Zebedee, and He began to be sorrowful and deeply distressed. Then He said to them, "My soul is exceedingly sorrowful, even to death. Stay here and watch with Me." He went a little farther and fell on His face, and prayed...

Matt 26:36-39 (NKJ)

Notice it says that Jesus, "went a little farther." Underline that phrase in your Bible. An extremist is one who leaves the realm of average and goes "a little farther." An extremist digs into the Word more than the average Christian and thus, lives a more abundant life.

John 10:10 says, *"...I have come that they may have life, and that they may have it more abundantly."* (NKJ)

You can get by with life, or you can go "a little farther" and have life more abundantly. It's up to you.

Hyper-Faith Paranoia

I was born and raised in Tulsa, Oklahoma. It was a great place to grow up because it was the governing city for the Word of Faith movement. At the time, all the preachers I admired were being called "hyper-faith" preachers.

"Watch out for those hyper-faith preachers," people would say. "Be careful of Kenneth E. Hagin, be careful of Kenneth Copeland and be careful of Oral Roberts — they go too far."

It's interesting that those who screamed the loudest against the faith preachers are no longer around but those who preached faith are still paying their bills and increasing every year!

I like how Dr. Lester Sumrall would respond when he was asked if he was a hyper-faith preacher. He would say, "I'm hyper, supersonic, bionic, nuclear and every other kind of faith there is. I want every kind of faith that exists so I can conquer the world for the Lord!"

Yes, I'm A Prosperity And Health Preacher!

After a service one time, the relatives of one of my students stopped me in the foyer of the church and wanted to ask me some questions. Questions don't bother me because I have nothing to hide. Everything I've ever preached is recorded, videotaped, and printed. If you want to know what I've said, it's available somewhere.

"Are you one of those prosperity and health preachers?" they asked.

By the way they said it, I knew they were against it, so I decided to be creative in my response.

"Before I answer you, let me ask you a question. If I gave an altar call this morning and said, 'all those who want blindness to come to the left side of this platform, and all those who want AIDS, and leukemia come to the right;' would you want your sister to come to my Bible school or go to my church?"

I was trying to win them over to thinking straight; not to my side, but to what the Word says.

"You don't understand what we're asking," they replied.

"Yes I do. You think I'm out of balance if I believe it's God's will to heal and to help everybody."

"Welllllllll," they said.

"Before you go any farther," I interrupted, "let me answer your other question. You asked if I was a prosperity preacher. What if you came to my midweek service and I said, 'All those who want to give God extra glory this week, I'm going to pray that God will give you lack, poverty and financial depression. Come to the altar real fast and God will bless you mightily,' Would you want your sister to come and be a part of that?"

They just looked at me.

"Then my answer is yes, I'm a health and prosperity preacher! If you want to be sick, broke and poor, then don't come to my church!"

Don't Be Nice To Sickness And Poverty

You had better watch what you're saying because you may be saying something you honestly don't want to receive. It's popular in many places to be anti-faith, anti-healing and anti-abundant life.

"Well, I don't want to be a prosperity person!"

Be a broke person then!

"Brother Roberts, you don't sound very nice!"

I'll *never* be nice to those kinds of attitudes! I hate them because they're from the devil!

From Glory To Glory

Being an extremist doesn't mean that you go into your own little world or become a lonely sheepherder. It just means you grow stronger in faith and you dig deeper into the Bible. It means you go a little farther into the things of God than the average Christian. This is how God continuously reveals His standard to His people. This is how He takes the church from glory to glory. He uses people who are willing to go beyond what is considered socially acceptable.

3

What Is A Radical?

In Matthew 22:37 we have the scriptural definition of the word, Radical.

"...You shall love the Lord your God with all your heart, with all your soul, and with all your mind. This is the first and great commandment." (NKJ)

Underline the word all. Radicals are those who love the Lord with *all* their heart, soul and mind, not just part of it.

Before he died, Keith Green said, "A radical is somebody who loves Jesus more than you." I like that definition.

When you're a radical, you love Jesus more than the average Christian. When you run into someone who doesn't love Jesus with all their heart, soul, mind and strength, they will react to you in one of two ways. They will either feel convicted and begin to love Jesus more, or they will defend their own backslidden condition and accuse you of being too radical.

Unexpected Surprises In Sweden

When I lived in Tulsa, I thought I was on the cutting edge of everything God was doing in the earth. We knew how to bind and loose — we knew how to get people healed. I was sure that we were the most radical Christians around. After stepping into ministry, I found out how wrong I was.

I was invited to preach at a Bible college in Uppsala, Sweden by a pastor named Ulf Eckman. I showed up wearing my little Tulsa suit, I had my little Tulsa walk and I had my little Tulsa attitude.

When I arrived, there were 450 blond-headed Bible students singing to God on their tippy-toes, with both hands in the air. Even their fingers were stretched out as far as they could stretch. During the praise songs they would jump up and down real fast and when it was worship time, they would cry and weep from the innermost depths of their heart. I had never seen anything like this in my life.

The presence of God was everywhere in that place; under the chair, on the platform, behind the curtains — everywhere! I even felt His presence when I went to the bathroom to wash my hands!

I thought, "What is this?"

During the praise and worship, there was such a unity amongst them; I felt like the odd duck in the row. They had a flow that I was not used to. Nevertheless, the Holy Spirit was with them in a mighty way.

Three Punches That Changed My Life

I preached there four days. On the last day, the Lord laid on my heart to pray for all the students. When I laid my hands on them and prayed, they fell out and shook.

Then Ulf approached me and said, "Can I pray for you?"

"Sure," I said, not realizing that I was totally unprepared for what was about to happen.

Suddenly, Ulf grabbed my head and my belly, and began groaning loudly in the Spirit (Rom. 8:26). Before I knew it, I was flat on the floor! He got down there with me and began to pray in depths of the Spirit that I could never explain to you. I had never heard anything like this! He had a groan in the Holy Ghost that sounded like a live tiger in front of me!

I opened my eyes just in time to see Ulf put his fist together and aim for my head! He hit me three times and I never felt one of them!

Bam! Bam! Bam!

Each time he hit me, a holy groan and travail came up out of his spirit.

While we were on the floor, all 450 students stretched out both hands toward us and prayed in strong tongues. If I had not been a wild person myself, I'd have gotten scared and run away!

Learn To Receive From Anybody

When I flew home that afternoon, I knew that something was different — I had received something from God. Before that conference, I thought I was free — I thought I was a real radical. But after they got through praying for me, I realized I wasn't that hot at all; I was just semi-warm!

There are times when you don't realize you're bound till you get free. I know that sounds kind of strange, but it's true. I was one of those. I had my Tulsa thing down and I thought I was doing pretty good. Well my brother and sister, I woke up.

Thank God I learned how to receive from anybody. I don't care if they're, young, old, American, Scandinavian,

Asian, or African; If they have more of God than me, I'll receive from them. You should have that attitude too.

No Reservations

To be a radical means that you love God with all your being. It means that you obey Him with no reservations or impure motives. You can't say, "I'll obey you Lord if You'll do this for me." No, no, no! It doesn't work like that! If you want to be a true radical, you have to give your all to God with no reservations. When you give your all, God's all will come to you.

A radical is not some isolated weirdo — it's just somebody who loves God a little more than you. A radical church is one that takes God's Word a little more serious than the average church. A radical preacher is somebody who takes God's commissions a little more serious than the average preacher. When you meet those kinds of people, you'll either be provoked to do more, or, you'll criticize them and defend where you're at.

Let's be the one that says, "I want what they have," and then do what it takes to get it.

4

What Is A Non-Conformist?

I heard the word non-conformist used for the first time while I was in London. I had a day off and I decided to go hunting for rare Christian books.

If you're going to send me a gift, don't send me an ornament, send me an old book. Old Christian books make me real happy. If you want to make my day, send me one by Wesley, or Spurgeon, or someone like that — I'll feel like I've gone to heaven.

Anyway, I heard about a Methodist church in London that had been closed and converted into a used book store.

I figured it would be full of old books by famous Christian authors, so I went to check it out. When I arrived, I asked a fellow at the counter if he had any books by John Wesley.

"Who?"

"You're standing in a building that Wesley's movement built and you don't know who Wesley is?" I said.

I was a little disgusted with the man.

"Oh, the non-conformist people," he responded with a condescending tone, "They're in the far back, on those last few shelves."

As I walked to the back, I thought, if a non-conformist is somebody that doesn't conform, then that was not quite true of Wesley. Wesley did conform. He conformed to the image of Christ. They just called him a non-conformist because he refused to conform to the dead religiosity of his day.

The Prophet Who Refused To Conform

There is a story I like in the Old Testament about a certain prophet who faced the pressure to conform. In 1 Kings 22:6-27, we find that the king of Israel had gathered his prophets to inquire of the Lord through them.

"Shall I go up against Ramoth Gilead to fight," he asked, "or shall I refrain?"

And all the king's pillow prophets responded by saying, "Go up, for the Lord will deliver it into your hand!"

Then Jehoshaphat, the king's associate in battle said, "Something doesn't seem right here. Isn't there anybody else we can ask?"

"Well, there's one other prophet named Micaiah," answered the King, "but I don't like him, because all he does is prophesy bad things about me. In fact, I hate him."

Jehoshaphat said, "We should hear from him anyway."

So they sent a servant to get the prophet.

The servant found Micaiah and said, "All the other prophets have told the king to go to war. Why don't you say the same thing? It would be nice to have a unified prophetic front."

So Micaiah stood to address the king.

"Go up to war and prosper," he said with a sigh.

But the king suspected that Micaiah was not telling him the truth. "No, tell me what the Lord is really saying!"

"Well, since you pressed the point," replied Micaiah, "the Lord showed me that the people of Israel are scattered everywhere like sheep with no shepherd!"

"See, didn't I tell you that Micaiah has nothing good to say about me!" the king said to Jehoshaphat.

Then they slapped Micaiah and imprisoned him, all because he gave them the Word of the Lord.

Micaiah was a non-conformist. He didn't conform to the religious pressure of his day.

The Scriptural Definition Of Non-Conformist

In Romans 12:1-2, the Apostle Paul gives us the scriptural definition of the word non-conformist. He writes:

I beseech you therefore, brethren, by the mercies of God, that you present your bodies a living sacrifice, holy, acceptable to God, which is your reasonable service.

Notice Paul didn't say, "a dead sacrifice!" He said, "a living sacrifice," so don't act like a dead one!

The only problem with a living sacrifice is that sometimes they crawl off the altar. To be a living sacrifice, you need to stay on the altar and let God burn up what needs to be burnt up and add what needs to be added.

And do not be conformed to this world, but be transformed by the renewing of your mind, that you may prove what is that good and acceptable and perfect will of God. (NKJ)

Here Paul tells us to be non-conformists. He tells us not to conform to the prince of the air or to the social ills of our time. Instead, we are to be transformed into the image of Christ.

We should love being called non-conformists. We don't conform to the ignorance, to the rebellion, to the lack of morals in our society, to the loss of common sense, to the loss of love or the loss of right relationship with our fellow friends. We're not going to conform to deviate sex, and say it's normal.

"Well, you're not being open."

That's right. I want to keep myself together.

"Well, Christians are close minded."

Yes, and that's why we think straight. We won't let anyone move us away from conforming to the image of God's dear Son. We want to walk like Jesus and talk like Jesus; we want to become the spitting image of Jesus Christ.

Christians *are* a conforming people. We just don't conform to homosexual weirdism or to the occultism of our time. We are against these things on purpose. That's why we're here.

"So, you're a non-conformist?"

Yes, and you should be too!

Martin Luther

Martin Luther was a non-conforming Catholic priest in Germany who stood up one day and said, "I think there should be some changes around here."

The first time the Pope heard about Luther, he said, "Oh, it's just a drunk priest." The second time he heard about Luther, he said, "Oh, it's just the other priests. They are jealous of him and making bad stories." The third time the Pope said, "Excommunicate him."

If Luther would have been your average Catholic priest, we'd still be listening to the scriptures in Latin. We would still be trying to pay for our relatives to get out of Purgatory and go to Heaven. If Luther hadn't refused to conform and gone a little farther toward the light, we would still be living in the dark ages.

Luther fought for the truth. He refused to compromise his stand and bow to the opposition. He was a non-conformist who changed the world and what he stands for is still being used to change the world today.

John Wesley

John Wesley, was one of the greatest non-conformists of Great Britain. If he had conformed to the spirit of the 1700s, all the revolutionary wars that were taking place in France and the other European countries would have crossed the English Channel and come into England. There would have been a blood bath. Wesley resisted the evil of his day and stopped the warring hordes from entering England. Instead of a blood bath, the people were washed in the blood of Christ. Wesley's refusal to conform saved England and caused its social climate to be lifted.

What if he had conformed? England would have lost thousands and she probably would not be where she's at today.

So let's not be conformed to the spirit of this age. Let's conform to the image of God's dear Son. The next time someone accuses you of being one of those fundamental Bible stomping kind of Christians, say, "Yeah, I'm guilty, and I'm proud of it too!"

5

A New Generation Of Extremists, Radicals & Non-Conformists

Some of you reading this book have a call on your life. God has a great anointing for you to carry. When you begin to step into the fullness of your call, many will love and cherish you. Some will even pray for you and give their hard-earned money to support you. But there will also come those who will seek your destruction. Even some who wear a cross will attack you and accuse you of going too far. May you always remember that Jesus also went a little farther.

Some will say that you give too much of yourself or that you show too much love. Yet the Bible says we're to be a radical people and give our all to Him.

Others will ridicule you for always seeming to stand on the opposite end of public opinion. Yet the Bible says that we are a non-conformist people; we are not to conform to the weakness of our time, but to the strength of our God.

Joy Comes When We Give Our All

North America needs extremists, radicals and non-conformists. American churches have lost their edge because they're trying to find favor among the wrong kind of people. God is the only One we should want favor from.

It's not wrong to be called an extremist if you're going a little bit farther in faith, prayer and reaching souls for Jesus. It's not wrong to be called a radical when you've given your all to God. It's not wrong to be accused of always taking the opposing opinion when you're standing upon chapter and verse for your generation.

A New Breed Of Reformers And Revivalists

The next wave of reformers and revivalists will not be ashamed of the words: *extremist, radical* and *non-conformist.* We will not be afraid to be counted among the great men and women of God who were also called these things.

Luther was called a heretic and yet God awarded him great honor in Heaven because he broke the religious control of his day. John Knox broke religious control in Scotland; Wesley broke it in England and Whitefield broke it here in America. Thank God for people like that who said, "We'll not be your average British minister, we'll not be your average Catholic priest and we'll not be your average Scottish clergyman."

Let's be the generation who goes a little farther. Let's be the generation that is louder and bolder than the rest. Yes, we might be called extremists, radicals and nonconformists, but we'll be in good company.

Prayer

"Father, we thank you for this word of challenge. May it help those reading this book to quit being an average church member. May they step up and go farther into what they are called to do. I speak change into the hearts of these people. I speak prophetic movements into the hearts of these people. Let there be new zeal and let there be new light in the hearts of these people. I break religious control, I break atmospherical manipulation. I release new freedom for the right causes. I release that into the hearts of these readers, in the Name of Jesus." Amen.

BOOKS

by Roberts Liardon

A Call To Action

Cry Of The Spirit

Extremists, Radicals and Non-Conformists

Final Approach

Forget Not His Benefits

God's Generals

Haunted Houses, Ghosts, And Demons

Holding To The Word of The Lord

I Saw Heaven

Kathryn Kuhlman

Knowing People By The Spirit

On Her Knees

Religious Politics

Run To The Battle

School of The Spirit

Sharpening Your Discernment

Smith Wigglesworth - Complete Collection

Smith Wigglesworth Speaks To Students

Spiritual Timing

The Invading Force

The Most Dangerous Place To Be

The Price of Spiritual Power

The Quest For Spiritual Hunger

Three Outs and You're In

*To place an order call (949) 833-3555
or visit our website at: www.robertsliardon.org*

Spirit Life Partner

Wouldn't It Be Great...

- If you could feed over 1,000 hungry people every week?
- If you could travel 250,000 air miles, boldly preaching the Word of God in 93 nations?
- If you could strengthen and train the next generation of God's leaders?
- If you could translate 23 books and distribute them into 37 countries?

Project Joseph Food Outreach.

...Now You Can!

Maybe you can't go, but by supporting this ministry every month, your gift can help to communicate the gospel around the world.

---------------------| CLIP ALONG LINE & MAIL TO ROBERTS LIARDON MINISTRIES. |---------------------

☐ **YES!!** Pastor Roberts, I want to support your work in the kingdom of God by becoming a **SPIRIT LIFE PARTNER.** Please find enclosed my first monthly gift.

Name _____

Address _____

City _____ State _____ Zip _____

Phone (_____) _____

SPIRIT LIFE PARTNER AMOUNT: $ _____

☐ Check / Money Order   ☐ VISA   ☐ American Express   ☐ Discover   ☐ MasterCard

☐☐☐☐☐ ☐☐☐☐ ☐☐☐☐ ☐☐☐☐

Name On Card _____ Exp. Date ___/___/___

Signature _____ Date ___/___/___

Roberts Liardon Ministries

P.O. Box 30710 ♦ Laguna Hills, CA 92654 ♦ (949) 833-3555 ♦ Fax (949) 833.9555 ♦ www.robertsliardon.org

AUDIO TAPES *by Roberts Liardon*

Acts of The Holy Spirit
Be Strong In The Lord
Breaking the Cycle of Failure
Changing Spiritual Climates
God's Secret Agents
Haunted Houses, Ghosts, & Demons
How To Combat Demonic Forces
How To Stay On The Mountaintop
How To Stir Up Your Calling
    and Walk In Your Gifts
How To Survive An Attack
Increasing Your Spiritual Capacity
I Saw Heaven
Life & Ministry of Kathryn Kuhlman
Living On The Offensive
No More Religion
Obtaining Your Financial Harvest
Occupy 'Til He Comes
Personality of the Holy Spirit
Prayer 1 - How I Learned To Pray
Prayer 2 - Lost In The Spirit
Reformers & Revivalists
Rivers of Living Water (Grams)
School of The Spirit
Seven Steps of Demonic Posession
Sharpening Your Discernment (One)
Sharpening Your Discernment (Two)

Spirit Life
Spiritual Climates
Storms of His Presence
Taking A City
Tired? How To Live In The
    Divine Life of God
True Spiritual Strength
The Anointing
The Healing Evangelists
The Charges of St. Paul - 1 Timothy
The Charges of St. Paul - 2 Timothy
The Working of Miracles
    & Divine Health
Three Arenas of Authority
    & Conflict
Three Worlds: God, You,
    & The Devil
Tired? How To Live In The
    Divine Life Of God
Tongues And Their Diversities
True Spiritual Strength
Useable Faith
Victorious Living In The Last Days
Working The Word
What You Need To Keep
    Under To Go Over
Your Faith Stops The Devil

To place an order call (949) 833-3555
or visit our website at: www.robertsliardon.org

Seven reasons you should attend Spirit Life Bible College

1. SLBC is a **spiritual school** with an academic support; not an academic school with a spiritual touch.

2. SLBC teachers are **successful ministers** in their own right. Pastor Roberts Liardon will not allow failure to be imparted into his students.

3. SLBC is a member of **Oral Roberts University Educational Fellowship** and is **fully accredited** by the International Christian Accreditation Association.

4. SLBC hosts monthly seminars with some of the **world's greatest** ministers who add another element, anointing and impartation to the students' lives.

5. Roberts Liardon understands your commitment to come to SLBC and commits himself to students by **ministering weekly** in classroom settings.

6. SLBC provides **hands-on** ministerial training.

7. SLBC provides ministry opportunity through its **post-graduate placement program**.

CLIP ALONG LINE & MAIL TO ROBERTS LIARDON MINISTRIES.

☐ **YES!!** Pastor Roberts, I am interested in attending **SPIRIT LIFE BIBLE COLLEGE**. Please send me an information packet.

Name _____

Address _____

City _____ State _____ Zip _____

Phone (_____) _____

Roberts Liardon Ministries
P.O. Box 30710 ♦ Laguna Hills, CA 92654
(949) 833-3555 ♦ Fax (949) 833.9555
www.robertsliardon.org

VIDEO TAPES *by Roberts Liardon*

2+2=4

And The Cloud Came

A New Generation

Apostles, Prophets
    & Territorial Churches

Apostolic Alignment

Are You A Prophet?

Confronting The Brazen Heavens

Developing An Excellent Spirit

Don't Break Rank

Does Your Pastor Carry A Knife?

Forget Not His Benefits

God's Explosive Weapons

How To Be An End Time Servant

How To Be Healed
    of Spiritual Blindness

I Saw Heaven

Ministering To The Lord

No More Walls

Reformers And Revivalists (5 Vol.)

Spirit of Evangelism

The Importance of Praying
    In Tongues

The Lord Is A Warrior

The Most Dangerous Place To Be

The New Millennium Roar

The Operation of Exhortation

The Word of The Lord Came
    Unto Me Saying

True And False Manifestations

Was Jesus Religious?

Why God Wrote Verse 28

New God's Generals Video Collection

Volume 1 - John Alexander Dowie

Volume 2 - Maria Woodworth-Etter

Volume 3 - Evan Roberts

Volume 4 - Charles F. Parham &
    William J. Seymour

Volume 5 - John G. Lake

Volume 6 - Smith Wigglesworth

Volume 7 - Aimee Semple
    McPherson

Volume 8 - William Branham

Volume 9 - Jack Coe

Volume 10 - A. A. Allen

Volume 11 - Kathryn Kuhlman

Volume 12 - Highlights
    & Live Footage

Videos by Gladoylene Moore (Grams)

Foundations of Stone

God of the Breakthrough

How I Learned To Pray

How To Avoid Disaster

Seeking God

The Prophetic Flow

The Sword Of Gideon

The Warrior Names of God

*To place an order call (949) 833-3555
or visit our website at: www.robertsliardon.org*

ROBERTS LIARDON MINISTRIES INTERNATIONAL OFFICES

EUROPE
Roberts Liardon Ministries
P.O. Box 2043
Hove, Brighton
East Sussex, BN3 6JU
England
011-44-1707-327-222

SOUTH AFRICA
Roberts Liardon Ministries
P.O. Box 3155
Kimberely 8300
South Africa
011-27-53-832-1207

AUSTRALIA
Roberts Liardon Ministries
P.O. Box 7
Kingsgrove, NSW
1480
Australia
011-61-500-555-056

Roberts Liardon Ministries

P.O. Box 30710
Laguna Hills, California, USA
92654-0710
Telephone: (949) 833-3555
Fax: (949) 833-9555
Visit our website at: www.robertsliardon.org